MUSEUM Colors

First Edition
Printed in China

10 09 08 07   10 9 8 7 6 5 4 3 2

Produced by the Department of Special Publications, The Metropolitan Museum of Art:
Robie Rogge, Publishing Manager; Jessica Schulte, Project Editor; Anna Raff, Designer; Gillian Moran, Production Associate.

All photography by The Metropolitan Museum of Art Photograph Studio
Visit the Museum's website: www.metmuseum.org

ISBN 1-58839-183-3

Library of Congress Cataloging-in-Publication Data

Metropolitan Museum of Art (New York, N.Y.)
    Museum colors : the Metropolitan Museum of Art.-- 1st ed.
        p. cm.
    ISBN 1-58839-183-3
    1. Color in art--Juvenile literature. 2. Metropolitan Museum of Art (New York,
N.Y.)--Juvenile literature. I. Title.
    N7432.7M48 2006
    701'.85--dc22
                                                            2006005685

MUSEUM Colors

THE METROPOLITAN MUSEUM OF ART
New York

What color are the bananas?

yellow

What color is the necklace?

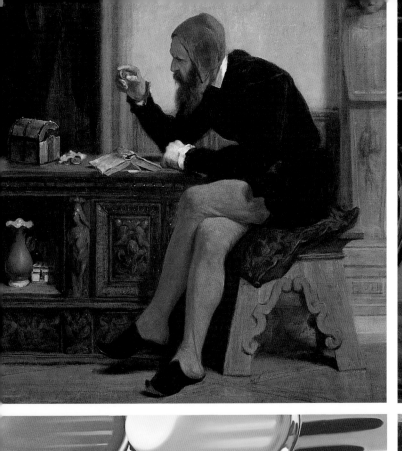

red

What color is the sky?

blue

What color is the melon?

orange

What color are the plums?

purple

What color are the trees?

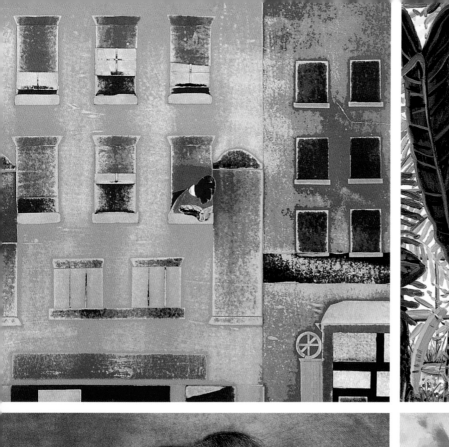

green

What color are the lady's lips?

pink

What color are the eggs?

white

What color is the sea?

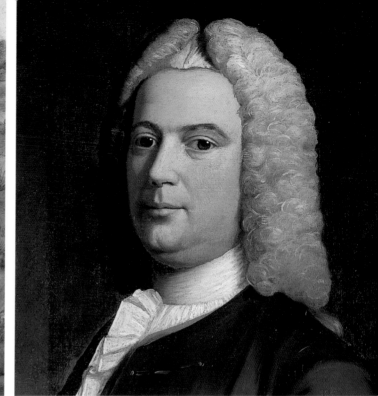

gray

What color is the dress?

black

The captions correspond to the pictures at the top of each column, reading clockwise from top left.

YELLOW

Basket of Bananas (detail)
Pierre Bonnard, French, 1867–1947
Oil on canvas, 23⅜ x 25¼ in., 1926
Jacques and Natasha Gelman Collection, 1998
1999.363.7

Evening Glow at Nihonbashi (detail)
Keisai Eisen, Japanese, 1790–1848
From the series *Eight Views of Edo*
Polychrome woodblock print, 9 x 14 in., ca. 1840
Rogers Fund, 1922   JP 1283

Small Daffodils (detail)
Charles Demuth, American, 1883–1935
Watercolor and pencil on paper, 13¾ x 10 in., ca. 1914
Alfred Stieglitz Collection, 1949   49.70.63

Merengue en Boca Chica (detail)
Rafael Ferrer, American (b. Puerto Rico), b. 1933
Oil on canvas, 60 x 72 in., 1983
Purchase, Anonymous Gift, 1984   1984.2

Rank Badge (detail)
Chinese, Qing dynasty, late 18th–early 19th century
Embroidered silk, 12¾ x 12½ in.
Anonymous Gift, 1946   46.133.54

RED

Portrait of a Woman (detail)
Domenico Ghirlandaio (Domenico di Tommaso
Curradi di Doffo Bigordi), Italian (Florentine),
1449–1494
Tempera on wood, 22½ x 17⅝ in.
The Friedsam Collection, Bequest of Michael
Friedsam, 1931 32.100.71

The Antiquary (detail)
Edwin White, American, 1817–1877
Oil on canvas, 22¼ x 27¼ in., 1855
Gift of Mrs. Edwin White, 1877   77.5

Raspberries and Goldfish (detail)
Janet Fish, American, b. 1938
Oil on canvas, 72 x 64 in., 1981
Purchase, The Cape Branch Foundation and Lila
Acheson Wallace Gifts, 1983   1983.171

Glowing Night (detail)
Oscar Bluemner, American (b. Germany), 1867–1938
Watercolor and pencil on paper, 9¼ x 12⅜ in., 1924
Bequest of Charles F. Iklé, 1963 64.27.10

House of Fire (detail)
James Rosenquist, American, b. 1933
Oil on canvas, 6 ft. 6 in. x 16 ft. 6 in., 1981
Purchase, Arthur Hoppock Hearn Fund, George A.
Hearn Fund and Lila Acheson Wallace Gift, 1982
1982.90.1a–c

BLUE

Fourteenth Street, High Noon (detail)
John Button, American, 1929–1982
Gouache on paper, 14⅛ x 20 in., 1977
Gift of Dr. and Mrs. Robert E. Carroll, 1979
1979.138.1

Old Souvenirs (detail)
John Frederick Peto, American, 1854–1907
Oil on canvas, 26¾ x 22 in., 1881
Bequest of Oliver Burr Jennings, 1968 68.205.3

*Plate Two from "Illustrations of Ancient Palanquins
and Carriages"* (detail)
Japanese, ca. 1899
Polychrome woodblock print, 14¼ x 10 in.
Gift of Lincoln Kirstein, 1970   1970.565.331

Edison Mazda (detail)
Stuart Davis, American, 1892–1964
Oil on cardboard, 24½ x 18⅝ in., 1924
Purchase, Mr. and Mrs. Clarence Y. Palitz Jr. Gift, in
memory of her father, Nathan Dobson, 1982   1982.10

Tile Panel (detail)
Syrian, 17th century
Composite body, polychrome painted under a transparent glaze, 22 x 33 in.
Rogers Fund, 1922   22.185.13a-f

ORANGE

Melon (detail)
Joseph Hirsch, American, 1910–1981
Oil on canvas, 13¾ x 16¼ in., 1962
Gift of Rita and Daniel Fraad, 1978   1978.509.7

Rustam Slays Isfandiar (detail)
Attributed to Qasim, son of 'Ali, Iranian (Tabriz),
Safavid period, ca. 1525–30
Leaf from the *Shahnama* of Shah Tahmasp
(1522–1576); colors, ink, silver, and gold on paper
Gift of Arthur A. Houghton Jr., 1970   1970.301.55

Autumn Ivy (detail)
Ogata Kenzan, Japanese, 1663–1743
Hanging scroll; color and ink on paper, 8¾ x 10⅞ in.,
18th century
The Harry G. C. Packard Collection of Asian Art, Gift
of Harry G. C. Packard and Purchase, Fletcher,
Rogers, Harris Brisbane Dick and Louis V. Bell Funds,
Joseph Pulitzer Bequest and The Annenberg Fund Inc.
Gift, 1975   1975.268.67

Divan Japonais (detail)
Henri de Toulouse-Lautrec, French, 1864–1901
Lithograph printed in four colors, 31¹³⁄₁₆ x 23¹⁵⁄₁₆ in.,
19th century
Bequest of Clifford A. Furst, 1958   58.621.17

Seventh Avenue and 16th Street, New York (detail)
Mark Baum, American, 1903–1997
Oil on canvas, 30 x 28 in., 1932
Edith C. Blum Fund, 1983   1983.122.2

PURPLE

Plums (detail)
John William Hill, American, 1812–1879
Watercolor, graphite, and gouache on off-white bristol
board, 7⅞ x 12 in., 1870
Gift of J. Henry Hill, 1882   82.9.1

Enjoying Cherry Blossom Viewing at Ueno (detail)
Yōshu Chikanobu, Japanese, 1838–1912
Triptych of polychrome woodblock prints,
14 x 28¼ in., 1887
Gift of Lincoln Kirstein, 1959   JP 3306

A Meeting (detail)
Attributed to Muhammad Zaman, Iranian, Safavid
period, 17th century
Leaf from a *Shahnama* manuscript
Colors, ink, silver, and gold on paper, 18½ x 11¼ in., 1696
Gift of Alexander Smith Cochran, 1913   13.228.17

The Dock (detail)
B. J. O. Nordfeldt, American, 1878–1955
Color woodblock print, 11 x 12 in., 1916
Mrs. B. J. O Nordfeldt, 1955   55.634.80

Magnolias and Irises (detail)
Louis Comfort Tiffany, American, 1848–1933
Tiffany Studios
Leaded Favrile glass, 60¼ x 42 in., ca. 1908
Anonymous Gift, in memory of Mr. and Mrs. A. B.
Frank, 1981   1981.159

GREEN

Women Picking Olives (detail)
Vincent van Gogh, Dutch, 1853–1890
Oil on canvas, 28⅝ x 36 in., 1889–90
The Walter H. and Leonore Annenberg Collection,
Gift of Walter H. and Leonore Annenberg, 1995,
Bequest of Walter H. Annenberg, 2002   1995.535

The Block (detail)
Romare Bearden, American, 1911–1988
Cut and pasted printed, colored, and metallic papers,
photostats, pencil, ink marker, gouache, watercolor, and
pen and ink on Masonite, 4 ft. x 18 ft., 1971
Gift of Mr. and Mrs. Samuel Shore, 1978   1978.61.1–6

The Conservatory (detail)
David Bates, American, b. 1952
Oil on canvas, 96 x 78 in., 1985
Purchase, Mrs. Jan Cowles, Virginia Cowles Kurtis and
Charles Cowles Gifts, in memory of Gardner Cowles,
1986   1986.71

Market Place (detail)
Andreé Ruellan, American, b. 1905
Oil on canvas, 28 x 42¼ in., 1939
George A. Hearn Fund, 1940   40.83

Peasant Mother and Child (detail)
Mary Cassatt, American, 1844–1926
Drypoint and aquatint printed in color, 11½ in x 9⅞ in.,
ca. 1894
H. O. Havemeyer Collection, Bequest of Mrs. H. O.
Havemeyer, 1929   29.107.97

 **PINK**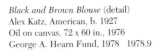

  WHITE

 **GRAY**

Black and Brown Blouse (detail)
Alex Katz, American, b. 1927
Oil on canvas, 72 x 60 in., 1976
George A. Hearn Fund, 1978   1978.9

Saint Dominic Resuscitating Napoleone Orsini (detail)
Bartolomeo degli Erri, Italian (Modenese), active
1460–79
Tempera on canvas, transferred from wood, 14 x 17½ in.,
1467–74
The Bequest of Michael Dreicer, 1921   22.60.59

Large Interior, Los Angeles (detail)
David Hockney, British, b. 1937
Oil, ink on cut-and-pasted paper, on canvas,
6 ft. ¼ in. x 10 ft. ¼ in., 1988
Purchase, Natasha Gelman Gift, in honor of William S.
Lieberman, 1989   1989.279

Mademoiselle V… in the Costume of an Espada
(detail)
Édouard Manet, French, 1832–1883
Oil on canvas, 65 x 50¼ in., 1862
H. O. Havemeyer Collection, Bequest of Mrs. H. O.
Havemeyer, 1929   29.100.53

The Demon Hiranyaksha Departs the Demon Palace
(detail)
Attributed to Manaku of Guler, Indian, ca. 1735–40
From a dispersed *Bhagavata Purana*
Ink, opaque watercolor, and gold on paper, 8⅝ x 12⅞ in.
Cynthia Hazen Polsky and Leon B. Polsky Fund, 2002
2002.179

Kitchen Scene (detail)
Peter Wtewael, Dutch, 1596–1660
Oil on canvas, 44¾ x 63 in.
Rogers Fund, 1906   06.288

Circus Equestrienne (detail)
Jean Metzinger, French, 1883–1956
Oil on canvas, 63¾ x 45 in., 1924
Gift of Nanette B. Kelekian, 2001   2001.556

*Omnia Vincit Amor, or The Power of Love in the Three
Elements* (detail)
Benjamin West, American, 1738–1820
Oil on canvas, 70⅜ x 80½ in., 1809
Maria DeWitt Jesup Fund, 1923   95.22.1

The Birches (detail)
Neil Welliver, American, 1929–2005
Oil on canvas, 60 x 60 in., 1977
Gift of Dr. and Mrs. Robert E. Carroll, 1979
1979.138.2

Relief of Nebhepetre Mentuhotep II (detail)
Egyptian, Middle Kingdom, Dynasty 11,
ca. 2051–2000 BC
Painted limestone, H. 14⅛ in.
Gift of Egypt Exploration Fund, 1907   07.230.2

The Lobsterman (The Doryman) (detail)
N. C. Wyeth, American, 1882–1945
Egg tempera on wood, 23¼ x 47¼ in., 1944
Gift of Amanda K. Berls, 1975   1975.322

Dervish and Bear (detail)
Indian, early 19th century
Leaf from the *Shah Jahan Album*
Ink, colors, and gold on paper, 15⅜6 x 10¼ in.
Purchase, Rogers Fund and The Kevorkian Foundation
Gift, 1955   55.121.10.9

Tench Francis (detail)
Robert Feke, American, ca. 1708–ca. 1751
Oil on canvas, 49 x 39 in., 1746
Maria DeWitt Jesup Fund, 1934   34.153

Deer and Monkeys in Landscape (detail)
Kawanabe Gyōsai, Japanese, 1831–1889
Album leaf; ink and color on silk, 14¼ x 10½ in.
Charles Stewart Smith Collection, Gift of Mrs. Charles
Stewart Smith, Charles Stewart Smith Jr. and Howard
Caswell Smith, in memory of Charles Stewart Smith,
1914   14.76.61.24

The Children of Nathan Starr (detail)
Ambrose Andrews, American, ca. 1801–1877
Oil on canvas, 28⅜ x 36½ in., 1835
Gift of Nina Howell Starr, in memory of Nathan
Comfort Starr (1896–1981), 1987   1987.404

BLACK

Madame X (Madame Pierre Gautreau) (detail)
John Singer Sargent, American, 1856–1925
Oil on canvas, 82⅛ x 43¼ in., 1883–84
Arthur Hoppock Hearn Fund, 1916   16.53

Martha Bartlett with Kitten (detail)
American, ca. 1875–1900
Oil on canvas, 30¼ x 24 in.
Bequest of Edgar William and Bernice Chrysler
Garbisch, 1979   1980.341.11

Young Woman Drawing (detail)
Marie-Denise Villers, French, 1774–1821
Oil on canvas, 63½ x 50⅝ in., 1801
Mr. and Mrs. Isaac D. Fletcher Collection, Bequest of
Isaac D. Fletcher, 1917   17.120.204

Khusrau and Shirin of Hafti (detail)
Turkish, Ottoman period, 1498–99
Ink, colors, and gold on paper; leather binding
Harris Brisbane Dick Fund, 1969   69.27

Women and Bird at Night (detail)
Joan Miró, Spanish, 1893–1983
Gouache on canvas, 9¼ x 16¾ in., 1944
Jacques and Natasha Gelman Collection, 1998
1999.363.54

yellow

red

blue

orange

purple

green

pink

white

gray

black